W9-CES-421

A TRUE BOOK™

Pluto
From Planet to Dwarf

ELAINE LANDAU

Children's Press®
A Division of Scholastic Inc.
New York   Toronto   London   Auckland   Sydney
Mexico City   New Delhi   Hong Kong
Danbury, Connecticut

Content Consultant

Michelle Yehling

Astronomy Education Consultant

Aurora, Illinois

Reading Consultant

Linda Cornwell

Literacy Consultant

Carmel, Indiana

Library of Congress Cataloging-in-Publication Data

Landau, Elaine.
Pluto : from planet to dwarf / by Elaine Landau.
   p. cm.—(A true book)
Includes bibliographical references and index.
ISBN-13: 978-0-531-12566-3 (lib. bdg.)   978-0-531-14794-8 (pbk.)
ISBN-10: 0-531-12566-1 (lib. bdg.)   0-531-14794-0 (pbk.)
1. Pluto (Dwarf planet)—Juvenile literature. I. Title. II. Series.
QB701.L355 2007
523.48'2—dc22   2007012279

All rights reserved. Published in 2008 by Children's Press, an imprint of Scholastic Inc.
Published simultaneously in Canada. Printed in China.
SCHOLASTIC, CHILDREN'S PRESS, A TRUE BOOK, and associated logos are trademarks and/or registered trademarks of Scholastic Inc.
2 3 4 5 6 7 8 9 10 R 17 16 15 14 13 12 11 10 09 08   62

Find the Truth!

Everything you are about to read is true *except* for one of the sentences on this page.

Which one is **TRUE**?

T or F   Pluto was named by an 11-year-old girl.

T or F   Pluto is a planet.

Find the answer in this book.

Contents

THE **BIG** TRUTH!

History of the Mystery

New Horizons

A person who weighs 100 pounds on Earth would weigh 7 pounds on Pluto.

Small, icy objects are found near Pluto's path around the sun.

The Hubble Space Telescope took this photo of Pluto and its three moons in 2006. The second-brightest object is Charon, the largest of Pluto's moons.

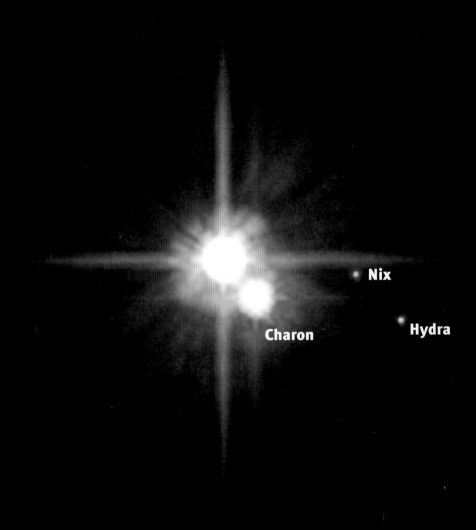

Nix

Charon

Hydra

CHAPTER 1

A Trip to Pluto

The Disney character Pluto, a dog, was named after the former planet.

For 76 years, most people thought of Pluto as our ninth planet. It was the smallest and coldest planet. And it was the planet farthest from the sun.

This is a drawing of Pluto and the sun. In reality, the sun would look much smaller from Pluto.

The Hubble Space Telescope weighs 24,500 pounds (11,110 kilograms). It travels around Earth once every 97 minutes.

Pluto never seemed the same as the other planets. **Astronomers** used to think that Pluto was the only object of its kind. Astronomers are scientists who study stars, planets, and space.

Today's astronomers have better **telescopes** to help them see clearly into space. They found other objects that looked similar to Pluto. Were these new discoveries planets too? Or was Pluto not a planet at all?

In August 2006, astronomers decided that Pluto was not a planet. They put Pluto into a new group called **dwarf planets**.

What would it be like to visit this faraway dwarf planet? Nobody knows for sure, because no one has ever been there. But astronomers do know some things about Pluto.

Pluto is about 3.6 billion miles (5.8 billion kilometers) from Earth. As you flew toward Pluto in a spaceship, the sun would get smaller behind you. By the time you arrived, the sun would only look like the brightest star in the sky.

It would take about 10 years for a spaceship to reach Pluto.

This drawing of Pluto (right) and Charon shows what you might see if you could travel to Pluto.

When you got close to Pluto, you would see
a light-brown ball with a lot of ice. You could
land your spaceship on its hard, icy surface. You
might also see a huge moon called Charon looming
above Pluto. It would look seven times bigger than
Earth's moon. Earth's moon seems to move across
the sky at night. But Pluto's moon would seem to
hang in one spot all night long.

This artwork shows the surface of Pluto with its moon Charon (right) and the sun (left) in the sky.

The sky is so dark on Pluto, you would see stars during the day!

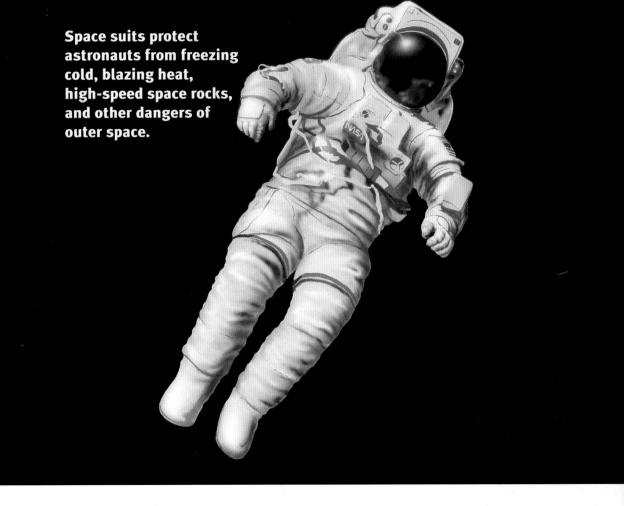

Space suits protect astronauts from freezing cold, blazing heat, high-speed space rocks, and other dangers of outer space.

You would need to wear a space suit to explore Pluto. A space suit would carry oxygen, a gas that humans need to breathe. There is no oxygen on Pluto. You wouldn't feel the sun's warmth out there. Pluto is extremely cold because it is so far from the sun.

Jupiter has 63 moons!

On its way to Pluto, *New Horizons* passed near Jupiter and some of its moons. In 2007, the spacecraft took this photograph of Io (left) and Europa (right), two of Jupiter's moons.

No spacecraft has ever visited Pluto. The first one to attempt it, called *New Horizons*, is still traveling on its way to Pluto. It will arrive in 2015. Only then will astronomers learn more about this mysterious dwarf planet.

Who Found Pluto?

Tiny Pluto was discovered because a young man named Clyde Tombaugh was looking hard for it.

Tombaugh wanted to be an astronomer. But he did not have money to pay for college. He built his own telescope and drew pictures of Mars and Jupiter. Tombaugh mailed his drawings to an **observatory**. Tombaugh got a job there looking for a new planet.

Night after night, Tombaugh took photographs of stars through a telescope. He searched the photographs for a planet. On February 18, 1930, Tombaugh discovered Pluto!

Clyde Tombaugh (right) knew Pluto was a planet because it moved across the sky. Tombaugh took the two photos (above) six days apart.

13

This image of Pluto (right) and its moon Charon (left) was taken by the Hubble Space Telescope in 1994. No telescope can get a clearer view of these two distant objects.

CHAPTER 2

Pluto in the Solar System

Seeing Pluto from Earth is like trying to see a walnut from 30 miles away.

Astronomers do not know as much about Pluto as they would like. It is too far away to see clearly, even with the most powerful telescopes. Still, astronomers have many tools to study this mysterious object. What they do know is that in many ways, Pluto is very different from the planets in our solar system.

Mercury Venus Earth Mars Jupiter

This image shows the order, and relative sizes, of the planets and Pluto in the solar system.

Our solar system has eight planets. They are Mercury, Venus, Earth, Mars, Jupiter, Saturn, Uranus, and Neptune. The dwarf planet Pluto is found beyond Neptune. The planets and dwarf planets **orbit**, or travel around, the sun.

Our solar system includes a lot of other things, too. Astronomers know of at least two other dwarf planets in our solar system. At least 162 moons orbit the planets and dwarf planets. Rocky **asteroids** and icy **comets** also orbit the sun.

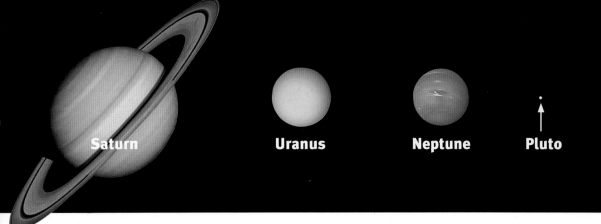

Saturn   Uranus   Neptune   Pluto

Rocky Planets, Gaseous Planets — and Pluto

Mercury, Venus, Earth, and Mars are terrestrial (tuh-RES-tree-uhl) planets. Terrestrial planets are hard, rocky planets with firm surfaces you could stand on. The four planets farthest from the sun are called gas giants. Jupiter, Saturn, Uranus, and Neptune are giant planets made mostly of gas and liquid.

Pluto is different. It is not rocky or near the sun like the terrestial planets. It is not large and full of liquid like the gas giants. Compared to the planets, Pluto is a small, distant ball of ice and rock.

This artwork shows a view from Pluto. The sun looks like a large star. Charon is on the horizon.

Pluto is so far from the sun that it is extremely cold. Astronomers think its temperature is about −375 degrees Fahrenheit (−226 degrees Celsius).

Pluto's icy surface is made up mostly of frozen chemicals other than water. Some of these chemicals are found on Earth, as well. Astronomers think Pluto may have a rocky core, or center, under its ice.

 When Pluto gets closer to the sun, some of its ice turns into gas.

Overly Oval

Each planet orbits the sun in an oval called an ellipse (ee-LIPS). The sun is at the center of the ellipse. The farther a planet is from the sun, the bigger its ellipse around the sun.

One full trip around the sun is a planet's or dwarf planet's year. It takes Earth 365 days to go around the sun once. But Pluto is about 39 times farther away from the sun than Earth is. So it takes Pluto a lot longer to finish its orbit. One year on Pluto equals about 248 Earth years.

Pluto's orbit is strange. Its ellipse is much more oval than that of the planets. Sometimes Pluto is closer to the sun than at other times.

Pluto's Solar System

← Pluto (dwarf planet)

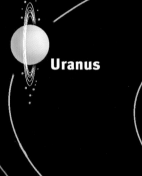

Uranus

Jupiter

Mars

Mercury

asteroid belt

Pluto

- Second dwarf planet from the sun
- Diameter: 1,422 mi. (2,288 km)
- Length of a day: About 6 days, 9 hours on Earth
- Length of a year: About 248 Earth years

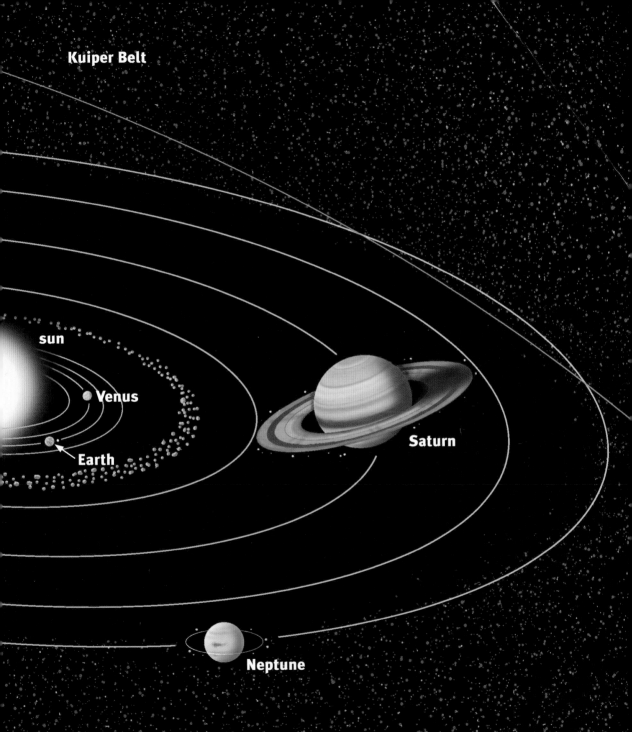

Kuiper Belt

sun

Venus

Earth

Saturn

Neptune

Pluto's Other Weird Ways

All planets and dwarf planets rotate, or spin, on an **axis**. An axis is an imaginary line that runs from north to south through the center of a planet. The time it takes a planet to rotate once equals one day on that planet. The dwarf planet Pluto takes more than six Earth days to rotate once on its axis.

 Pluto's axis is tilted so far that the planet is almost on its side.

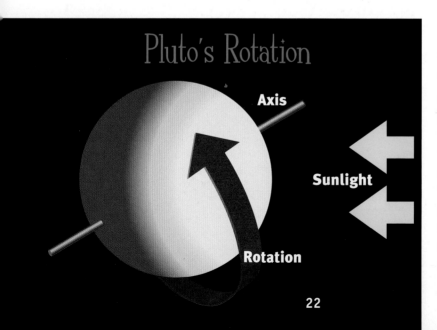

Pluto's Rotation

Axis

Sunlight

Rotation

The red arrow in this diagram shows the direction of Pluto's rotation. It is daytime on the side that faces the sun. As Pluto rotates, new areas move into the sunlight.

Sometimes Pluto is closer to the sun than Neptune.

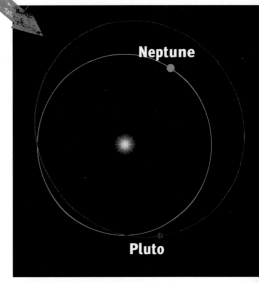

Pluto's strange orbit crosses Neptune's.

Astronomers think Pluto has an atmosphere like many of the planets in the solar system. An atmosphere is a blanket of gases that surrounds a planet or other space object. But Pluto's atmosphere forms only when its orbit brings it closer to the sun. Then there is enough heat from the sun to turn some of the ice on Pluto's surface to a gas. The gas forms a weak atmosphere on Pluto. When Pluto's orbit takes it farther from the sun, much of the gas freezes and falls back to the surface.

For a long time, most astronomers thought that Pluto could be this weird and still be called a planet. That changed after a big discovery.

In 1930, astronomers at Lowell Observatory used a 13-inch (33-centimeter) telescope to discover Pluto. These days, they use a 72-inch (1.8-meter) telescope. Larger telescopes usually give astronomers clearer views of space.

CHAPTER 3

Time for a Change

More than 70,000 people visit Arizona's Lowell Observatory every year.

For many years, few people questioned that Pluto was our ninth planet. Over time, astronomers invented better tools to study space. Powerful new telescopes were made. Astronomers began to see things that made them doubt that Pluto was a planet.

Pluto can be hard to find, even through a telescope.

Pluto

25

In 1992, astronomers spotted a small, rocky object even farther away than Pluto. Then a second object beyond Pluto was found. Then a third was found. One of these objects, Eris, is even bigger than Pluto!

Today, astronomers know of hundreds of these icy, rocky objects. They orbit the sun in a region of space beyond Neptune. Astronomers call this region the **Kuiper** (KY-pur) **Belt**. These objects are called **Kuiper Belt Objects**, or KBOs. Pluto is within this belt.

This image of Eris, the largest dwarf planet, was created on a computer.

This is an artist's vision of the Kuiper Belt.
KBOs are probably more spread out than shown here.

Many comets come from the Kuiper Belt.

Some astronomers began to wonder if Pluto was more like a KBO than a planet. As more KBOs popped up, so did more questions. Eris is the biggest KBO found so far. Should it be called a planet, too? What would happen if more large KBOs were discovered? Would the solar system have a huge number of planets?

What Is a Planet, Anyway?

Astronomers realized that they needed a good definition of a planet. So a large group of astronomers from around the world gathered for a meeting in August 2006. They agreed on a definition of a planet.

Now, to be a planet, an object must meet these three conditions:

- It has to orbit the sun.
- It has to have a nearly round shape.
- It has to "clear the neighborhood" around its orbit. This means that a planet has to get other space objects out of its path. How does a planet do this? It must have enough **gravity** to pull on objects and move them out of the way. Gravity is the force that pulls two objects together.

Dwarf planets can be KBOs, asteroids, or other kinds of space objects.

Pluto met two of these conditions. It orbits the sun. It is round. However, it doesn't have enough gravity to clear out its orbit. There are many other objects in the Kuiper Belt near Pluto's orbit.

Pluto could no longer be a planet. It was renamed a dwarf planet on August 24, 2006.

In 2006, members of the International Astronomical Union voted to name Pluto a dwarf planet.

1978

New photographs of Pluto reveal its moon Charon.

This background illustration shows the dwarf planet named Eris. The bright object at right is Eris's moon, Dysnomia.

1992

The first object in the Kuiper Belt is found.

2005

Eris and its moon, Dysnomia (dis-NOH-mee-uh), are found. Eris is nicknamed "the tenth planet." The Hubble Space Telescope spots two more moons around Pluto. They are named Nix and Hydra.

2006

Pluto is renamed a dwarf planet. Eris is named a dwarf planet, too. More than 800 Kuiper Belt Objects are found.

History of the Mystery

Tiny, icy, distant Pluto was hard to find. And it's been tricky to figure out how Pluto fits in the solar system. Here are some major steps in the study of Pluto.

1905
Astronomer Percival Lowell thinks there is a big planet beyond Neptune. He begins the search for Planet X.

1930
A man named Clyde Tombaugh works at Lowell Observatory looking for Planet X. While searching for Planet X, Tombaugh finds little Pluto instead!

1951
Astronomer Gerard Kuiper predicts that there are other small objects near Pluto.

In Roman mythology, Charon rowed people across a river to the underworld, or the land of the dead. The god Pluto ruled the underworld. This photo of Pluto and Charon was taken by the Hubble Space Telescope.

Pluto

Charon

CHAPTER 4

The Moons of Pluto

Astronomers first saw Charon 48 years after Pluto was discovered.

Pluto is unusual for yet another reason. Its largest moon is about half its size. Astronomers have never seen an object and its moon that were so close in size.

An artist drew this view of Pluto close to a KBO. A KBO probably would not come this close to Pluto.

Finding Charon

Pluto's largest moon is called Charon. It is so large compared to Pluto that they act like a pair. Moons orbit planets and other big objects because of gravity. Every object has gravity. The more massive the object, the more pull it has.

Because Pluto and Charon are close in size, they have a strong gravitational pull on each other. Therefore, they orbit each other. For this reason, Charon appears to stand still in Pluto's sky.

Charon was discovered in 1978 by James Christy. He noticed what looked like a bump on Pluto. The "bump" moved as Charon orbited Pluto.

Charon

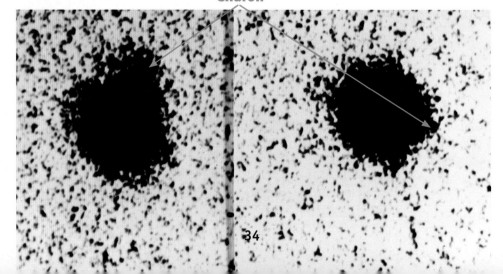

To Make a Moon

In some ways, Charon and Pluto are alike. Yet astronomers think that Charon's surface is different from Pluto's. Charon's ice is made of frozen water rather than other frozen materials.

An artist created this illustration of Pluto (above) and Charon (right) based on what astronomers know about these objects.

Astronomers have different ideas about how Charon may have formed. One idea is that a large object smashed into Pluto more than 4 billion years ago. Charon may have formed out of the materials that flew off during the crash. Some astronomers think that is also how Earth's moon was created.

Two More Moons

In 2005, astronomers using the Hubble Space Telescope discovered two more moons around Pluto. They are named Hydra (HY-druh) and Nix (NIKS). They are much smaller than Charon. Pluto may have more moons that have not yet been discovered. The first spacecraft to visit Pluto may do just that.

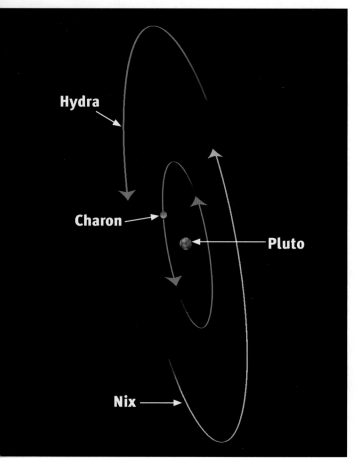

Hydra

Charon

Pluto

Nix

Astronomers think that Hydra and Nix are between 40 and 125 miles (64 and 200 km) in diameter.

The Name Game

Many objects in our solar system are named after characters from Greek or Roman myths. Pluto is the Roman god of the underworld, or the land of the dead.

An 11-year-old girl from Oxford, England, suggested the name Pluto. Venetia Burney chose a name that fit the idea of dark, cold space.

A friend of Venetia's family sent the idea to Lowell Observatory. Astronomers chose that name over others that were suggested. One reason was because both the god Pluto and the new space object were mysterious and hard to see. Another reason was that "PL" were the initials of Percival Lowell, the man who started the observatory that spotted Pluto.

Rejected Names for Pluto:

Constance	Lowell	Percival
Cronus	Minerva	Zeus

New Horizons was packed inside a cone to protect it during its trip through Earth's atmosphere. The cone was launched into space by a rocket.

CHAPTER 5

Mission to the Outer Limits

New Horizons and its rockets weighed more than 1 million pounds when they blasted off.

All eight planets have been studied up close by spacecraft. Pluto has not. But a space probe named *New Horizons* is now on its way to Pluto. A space probe is a spacecraft that doesn't have people on board.

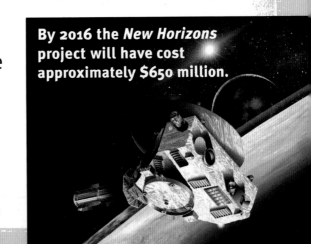

By 2016 the *New Horizons* project will have cost approximately $650 million.

New Horizons is a small, fast spacecraft. It began its long journey in early 2006. *New Horizons* will fly by Pluto and Charon in July 2015. The craft will send the first full-color close-up photos back to Earth. Instruments on the spacecraft may tell astronomers more about what Pluto and Charon are made of.

After passing Pluto and Charon, *New Horizons* will continue further into the Kuiper Belt. It may be able to study Kuiper Belt Objects there. Astronomers hope to learn more about how Pluto and Charon compare to these objects.

New Horizons will be flying at about 30,000 miles per hour when it reaches Pluto.

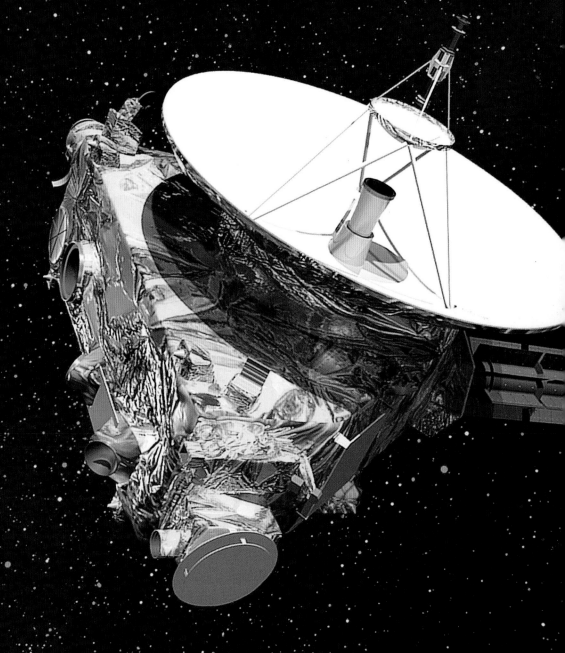

The ashes of Clyde Tombaugh, the man who discovered Pluto, were placed aboard the *New Horizons* spacecraft.

Pluto and Charon are on the edge of an exciting new frontier in the study of space. *New Horizons* promises to tell us more about the mysterious outer edges of our solar system. ⭐

An artist created this image of the Kuiper Belt.

True Statistics

Classification: Dwarf planet

Named after: Roman god of the underworld

Year discovered: 1930

Number of moons: At least 3

Atmosphere: Yes, sometimes

100-lb (45 kg) person on Earth would weigh: 7 lb. (3 kg)

Surface temperature: About –375ºF (–226ºC)

Distance from the sun: About 3.7 billion mi. (5.9 billion km)

Distance from Earth: About 3.6 billion mi. (5.8 billion km)

Length of a day: About 6 Earth days

Length of a year: About 248 Earth years

First mission: *New Horizons*, launched 2006

Did you find the truth?

T Pluto was named by an 11-year-old girl.

F Pluto is a planet.

Resources

Books

Atkinson, Stuart. *Space Travel*. Austin, TX: Raintree Steck-Vaughn, 2002.

Carruthers, Margaret. *The Hubble Space Telescope*. Danbury, CT: Franklin Watts, 2004.

Hansen, Rosanna. *Seeing Stars: The Milky Way and Its Constellations*. New York: Scholastic, 2002.

Prinja, Raman K. *Stars and Constellations*. Chicago: Heinemann Library, 2003.

Richardson, Adele. *Telescopes*. Mankato, MN: Capstone Press, 2004.

Shearer, Deborah A. *Space Missions*. Mankato, MN: Bridgestone Books, 2003.

Taylor-Butler, Christine. *Beyond Pluto*. Danbury, CT: Children's Press, 2007.

Taylor-Butler, Christine. *Pluto: Dwarf Planet*. Danbury, CT: Children's Press, 2008.

Vogt, Gregory. *Comets*. Mankato, MN: Bridgestone Books, 2002.

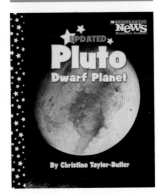

Organizations and Web Sites

National Space Society

1620 I Street NW, Suite 615
Washington, DC 20006
202-429-1600
This organization works toward having humans live and work in space.

New Horizons Mission

pluto.jhuapl.edu
Here you'll learn about the first space mission to Pluto and beyond.

Pluto: From Planet to Dwarf

www.space.com/pluto/
Check out this interesting Web site on Pluto and its moons.

Places to Visit

Kennedy Space Center

Kennedy Space Center, FL 32899
www.ksc.nasa.gov
Take a tour of KSC's giant rockets and launch pads.

Smithsonian National Air and Space Museum

Independence Avenue at 4th Street, SW
Washington, DC 20560
202-633-1000
www.nasm.si.edu
See the world's largest collection of historic airplanes and spaceships.

Important Words

asteroids (AS-tuh-roidz) – large pieces of rock that orbit the sun

astronomers – scientists who study planets, stars, and space

axis (AK-siss) – an imaginary line that runs from north to south through the center of a planet

comets – large chunks of rock and ice that travel around the sun

dwarf planets – bodies in the solar system that orbit the sun, have a constant (nearly round) shape, are not moons, and have orbits that overlap with the orbits of other bodies

gravity – a force that pulls two objects together

Kuiper Belt (KY-pur belt) – an area in the outer part of the solar system that contains thousands of small space objects

Kuiper Belt Objects – icy, rocky objects that orbit the sun in the distant Kuiper Belt

observatory – a building containing telescopes and other scientific instruments for studying space

orbit – to travel around an object such as a sun or planet

solar system – a sun and all the objects that travel around it

telescopes – instruments that make distant objects seem larger and closer; used especially to study subjects in space

Index

About the Author

Award-winning author Elaine Landau has a bachelor's degree from New York University and a master's degree in library and information science from Pratt Institute.

She has written more than 300 nonfiction books for children and young adults. Although Ms. Landau often writes on science topics, she especially likes writing about planets and space.

She lives in Miami, Florida, with her husband and son. The trio can often be spotted at the Miami Museum of Science and Space Transit Planetarium. You can visit Elaine Landau at her Web site: www.elainelandau.com.